BOSTON
BRUINS

BY WILLIAM ARTHUR

Book design by Maggie Villaume
Cover design by Maggie Villaume

Photographs ©: Nick Wass/AP Images, cover; Jonathan Hayward/The Canadian Press/AP Images, 4–5; Bob Frid/Icon Sportswire, 7; Julie Jacobson/AP Images, 9; AP Images, 10–11, 12–13, 15, 23; Dick Raphael/Sports Illustrated/Getty Images, 16–17; Ray Lussier/Boston Globe Out/Metro Boston Out/Boston Herald American/AP Images, 19; Susan Walsh/AP Images, 21; Jason Moore/ZUMA Press/Icon Sportswire, 24–25; Robin Alam/Icon Sportswire, 27; Bruce Bennett/Pool/AP Images, 29

Press Box Books, an imprint of Press Room Editions.

ISBN
978-1-63494-488-5 (library bound)
978-1-63494-514-1 (paperback)
978-1-63494-565-3 (epub)
978-1-63494-540-0 (hosted ebook)

Library of Congress Control Number: 2022902269

Distributed by North Star Editions, Inc.
2297 Waters Drive
Mendota Heights, MN 55120
www.northstareditions.com

Printed in the United States of America
082022

ABOUT THE AUTHOR

William Arthur is a lifelong hockey fan who grew up playing the sport on a frozen pond in Thunder Bay, Ontario. He lives in northwest Ontario with his trusted foxhound.

TABLE OF
CONTENTS

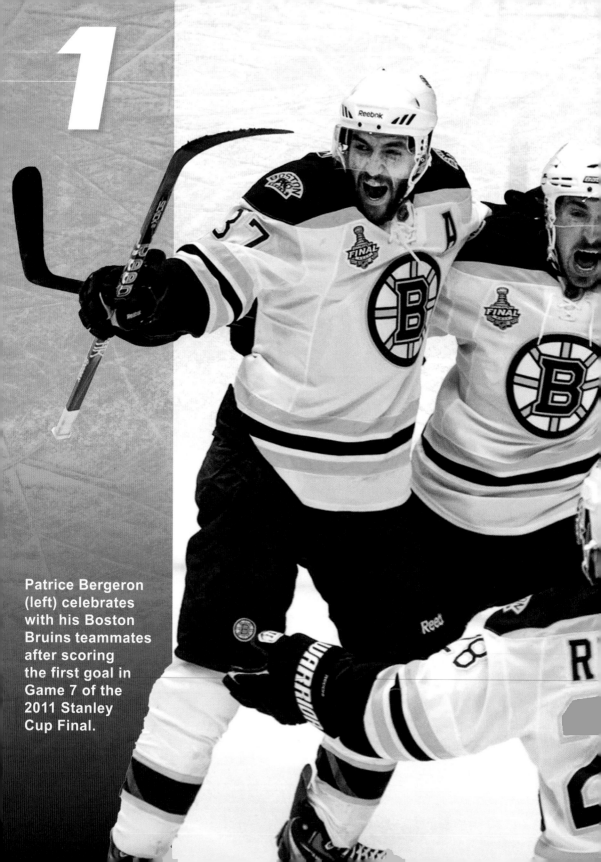

1

Patrice Bergeron (left) celebrates with his Boston Bruins teammates after scoring the first goal in Game 7 of the 2011 Stanley Cup Final.

BACK ON TOP

Boston Bruins rookie Brad Marchand skated with the puck along the boards. He spun around to escape a Vancouver Canucks defender. Then he flicked the puck to teammate Patrice Bergeron, who was waiting in front of the goal. Bergeron sent the puck into the back of the net. The Vancouver crowd fell silent. The Bruins had just taken a 1–0 lead in the first period.

Boston was playing at Vancouver in Game 7 of the 2011 Stanley Cup Final. In earlier rounds of the playoffs, the Bruins had won two Game 7s. Now they just needed one more.

Midway through the second period, Marchand collected a rebound next to the Canucks' net. Then he raced behind

•BRUINS VS. CANADIENS

The Bruins defeated the Montreal Canadiens in the first round of the 2011 playoffs. It was the latest chapter in one of hockey's fiercest rivalries. The Bruins and the Canadiens first met in 1924. They played every season after that until 2020–21. That year, teams played a limited number of opponents. The National Hockey League (NHL) created an unusual schedule because of the COVID-19 pandemic.

Bruins winger Brad Marchand completes a wraparound goal during Game 7 of the 2011 Stanley Cup.

the goal and scored on an incredible wraparound. Boston wasn't done yet. Five minutes later, on a penalty kill, Bergeron added a third goal.

Zdeno Chara, Boston's captain, anchored the team's defense. And anyone who got through Chara had to deal with Tim Thomas. The Bruins goalie saved nearly 97 percent of the Canucks' shots during the Final. Vancouver peppered him with shot after shot in Game 7. Time and time again, Thomas turned them away.

Many fans expected Game 7 to be a tight contest. In the Stanley Cup Final, three of the first six games had been decided by just one goal. But on this night, there was no stopping the Bruins.

Marchand sealed the victory with a late empty-net goal. When the final horn sounded, the Bruins players threw their gloves into the air. Fans back in Boston rejoiced, too. For the first time in 39 years, the Bruins were NHL champions.

Bruins captain Zdeno Chara hoists the Stanley Cup after winning the 2011 Final.

2

Bruins manager Art Ross (left) shakes Eddie Shore's hand after a game in 1934.

AMERICAN
ORIGINALS

Four Canadian teams came together in 1917 to form the NHL. Seven years later, the Boston Bruins became the league's first US team. Charles Francis Adams founded the team. He wanted its colors to be brown and yellow. Those colors were like the stores he owned.

Art Ross led the early Bruins teams. He held

Eddie Shore (center) helps defend during a 1938 game against the New York Rangers.

different roles for Boston until 1954. He coached the Bruins for 17 seasons. Ross also spent time as general manager.

One of his most successful moves was bringing in Eddie Shore. The skilled defenseman arrived in 1926. He became one of the sport's first true stars. Shore's

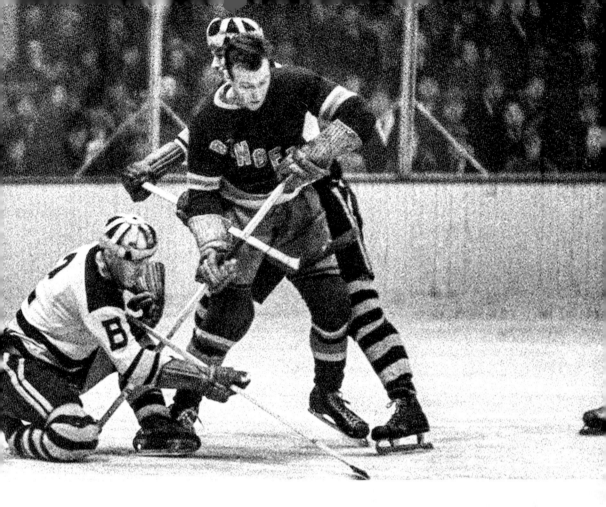

skating and stickhandling were top-notch.
But Shore was also tough and had no
problem racking up penalty minutes. He
led the Bruins to their first Stanley Cup
Final in 1927. Two years later, they won
their first championship. Boston swept the
New York Rangers in two games.

Shore helped the Bruins win a second Stanley Cup in 1939. By then, goalie Frank Brimsek had taken over as the team's star player. Two years later, in 1941, the Bruins won yet again.

The NHL saw lots of changes in its early years. Teams came and went. Then came the "Original Six" era. From 1942 to 1967, the same six teams made up the league. Many hockey fans look back

•CREATING AN IDENTITY

By the late 1930s, the Bruins' uniforms were black and yellow, as they still are today. The team had its 25th anniversary in 1948–49. To celebrate, the Bruins introduced a new logo. It featured a block B with spokes behind it. The design symbolized Boston's nickname, the Hub. A hub is a central point. Today the team's "spoked-B" logo is one of the most famous in North American sports.

Bruins captain Fern Flaman (right) battles with Jean Beliveau of the Montreal Canadiens during a 1958 game.

to this period fondly. The rivalries of the time became legendary. However, it was not a successful era for the Bruins. They were one of just two teams to never win a championship. But brighter days were just ahead.

3

Phil Esposito
makes a move
during a 1967
game.

GOLDEN STARS

The early 1960s marked a low point for the Bruins. But big changes were on the way. In 1966, the team signed a teenage defenseman named Bobby Orr. One year later, Boston traded for forwards Phil Esposito and Ken Hodge. And the team already had two stars in winger Johnny Bucyk and goalie Gerry Cheevers.

In 1968, the Bruins snapped an eight-year playoff drought. That had been the longest in team history. At the same time, they began a new streak. The Bruins went on to make 29 playoff appearances in a row. That set an NHL record.

Everything came together in 1970. The Bruins cruised through the playoffs. Then they opened the Stanley Cup Final with three wins over the St. Louis Blues. Game 4 went to overtime. Forty seconds later, Orr scored. Just as the puck went into the net, Orr was tripped. A photo of the airborne superstar became one of the most iconic in sports. More importantly, Boston had won another Stanley Cup.

Boston continued to enjoy huge success. Orr was one of the league's

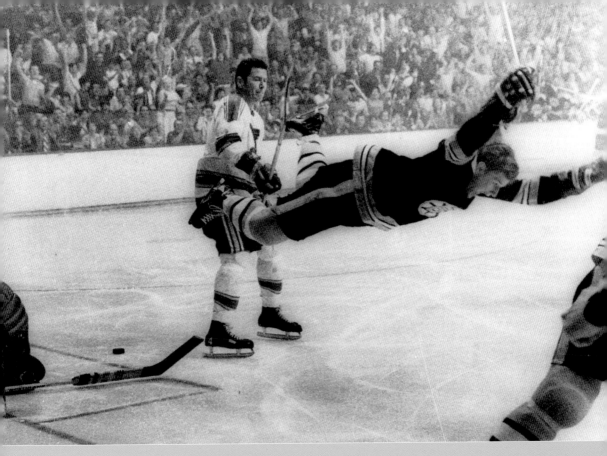

Bobby Orr soars through the air after winning the 1970 Stanley Cup.

best offensive players. He was also an elite defenseman. Meanwhile, Esposito routinely led the NHL in scoring. The pair led the Bruins to another Cup win in 1972. Boston reached three more Stanley Cup Finals in the decade. However, knee injuries cut Orr's career short. He played just 10 seasons in Boston.

Another franchise player was on his way, though. In 1979, the Bruins drafted defenseman Ray Bourque. For the next two decades, Bourque anchored Boston's blue line. In that time, he made 18 All-Star Games. Five times, he won the Norris Trophy as the league's best defenseman.

BIDDING ADIEU TO BOURQUE

By 1999, Bourque had played 20 seasons without winning a Stanley Cup. That streak looked like it would continue in 1999–2000. So, the Bruins traded him to the Colorado Avalanche. One year later, Bourque and the Avalanche won the Stanley Cup. The team captain typically lifts the Cup first. But Avalanche captain Joe Sakic gave the honor to Bourque. Bourque had played in a record 1,826 NHL games before winning his first championship. He later celebrated by bringing the Cup to Boston.

Ray Bourque shuts down a Detroit Red Wings player during a 1991 game.

And Bourque served as team captain for 15 seasons. The only thing Bourque didn't do before leaving in 2000 was win a Stanley Cup.

BOBBY ORR

Bobby Orr arrived in Boston as an 18-year-old in 1966. He quickly showed that defensemen could do much more than defend. Orr transformed the position. In fact, many people believe he was the best hockey player ever.

Orr was an unrivaled skater. He was as fast as they come. Yet he also knew just where to be. And when he got into the offensive zone, he was as dangerous as anyone. Orr led the league in assists five times. He scored at least 30 goals in each of those seasons. Orr won eight consecutive Norris Trophies as the NHL's top defenseman. He also won three Hart Trophies. That's the trophy for the most valuable player.

Perhaps the best measure of Orr's ability is his plus-minus. Orr was plus-574 over his career with the Bruins. Many fans believe his plus-124 rating from 1970–71 will never be beaten.

In 1969–70, Bobby Orr led the NHL
with 120 points. He became the first
defenseman to lead the league in scoring.

4

Zdeno Chara skates down the ice during a 2007 game.

STAYING STRONG

The Bruins' playoff streak ended in 1997. Over the next decade, they missed the postseason as often as they made it. The team needed a boost. In 2007, it got one.

Boston already had some solid players. That started with team captain Zdeno Chara. At 6-foot-9, the defenseman towered over opponents. Meanwhile, Patrice Bergeron and David Krejci were promising young forwards. But the Bruins needed a coach to bring that talent together. Claude Julien did just that.

Julien took over as coach before the 2007–08 season. A new playoff streak began right away. The Bruins won a playoff series in 2009 and another in 2010. Then, in 2011, they beat the Canucks to win the Stanley Cup.

By then, Brad Marchand had broken into the lineup. He was another skilled young forward. Meanwhile, Tim Thomas

•THE WINTER CLASSIC

In 2008, the NHL began hosting an outdoor game each year on January 1. The game is known as the Winter Classic. The 2010 game was held at Boston's Fenway Park. As of 2022, the Bruins had played in two other Winter Classics. They'd also played in one other outdoor game.

Brad Marchand handles the puck during Game 1 of the 2013 Stanley Cup Final.

and Tuukka Rask gave the Bruins a strong one-two punch in goal. The Bruins made another run to the Stanley Cup Final in 2013. However, they fell to the Chicago Blackhawks.

A new era began in February 2017. After missing the playoffs twice in a row, Julien was fired. Bruce Cassidy took over. Boston returned to the playoffs that season. Two years later, the team made another run. By then, young winger David Pastrnak had joined Bergeron and Marchand on Boston's top line. They led the Bruins all the way to the 2019 Stanley Cup Final. Unfortunately for Bruins fans, the team fell short again.

After 14 seasons, Chara left the team in 2020. Other longtime stars were getting older, too. Even so, the Bruins remained a top team in the Eastern Conference. After nearly a century of play, that was a position Boston knew well.

David Pastrnak scores against the St. Louis Blues during Game 6 of the 2019 Stanley Cup Final.

• BOSTON BRUINS
QUICK STATS

FOUNDED: 1924

STANLEY CUP CHAMPIONSHIPS: 6 (1929, 1939, 1941, 1970, 1972, 2011)

KEY COACHES:
- Art Ross (1925–34, 1936–39, 1941–45): 387 wins, 290 losses, 95 ties

- Claude Julien (2008–17): 419 wins, 246 losses, 94 overtime losses

HOME ARENA: TD Garden (Boston, MA)

MOST CAREER POINTS: Ray Bourque (1,506)

MOST CAREER GOALS: Johnny Bucyk (545)

MOST CAREER ASSISTS: Ray Bourque (1,111)

MOST CAREER SHUTOUTS: Tiny Thompson (74)

Stats are accurate through the 2020–21 season.

GLOSSARY

ASSISTS
Passes, rebounds, or deflections that result in goals.

CAPTAIN
A team's leader.

DRAFT
To select in an event that allows teams to choose new players coming into the league.

PANDEMIC
A disease that spreads quickly around the world.

PENALTY KILL
When one team has fewer players on the ice because someone is serving a penalty.

PLAYOFFS
A set of games to decide a league's champion.

PLUS-MINUS
A statistic that measures how many goals a team scored when a player was on the ice minus how many goals the team gave up.

REBOUND
When the goalie makes a save, but the puck goes back into play.

• TO LEARN
MORE

BOOKS

Croucher, Philip. *Brad Marchand: The Unlikely Star*. Halifax, NS: Nimbus Publishing, 2018.

Omoth, Tyler. *A Superfan's Guide to Pro Hockey Teams*. North Mankato, MN: Capstone Press, 2018.

Zweig, Eric. *Boston Bruins*. New York: Crabtree Publishing Company, 2018.

MORE INFORMATION

To learn more about the Boston Bruins, go to **pressboxbooks.com/AllAccess**.

These links are routinely monitored and updated to provide the most current information available.

INDEX